BY PLANE, TRAIN OR COINCIDENCE

by
Michele McDannold

ROADSIDE PRESS

Editor
Ezhno Martin

Foreword
Dan Denton

Roadside Press
200 W. Main St. Unit 209
Trinidad, Colorado 81082

Foreword by Dan Denton

A year ago, I re-read Michele McDannold's first poetry collection *Stealing the Moonlight from a Handful of Days* (Punk Hostage Press 2014). It is one of my favorite books of poetry. It's an in-your-face example of why I think Michele is one of the best living poets in America.

Soon as I finished re-reading that book, I heard another writer screw up Michele's name, and it irritated the fuck out of me. A year ago, I told Michele that I was going to figure out how to teach people to say her fucking name.

Michele McDannold. Let's all practice saying it together. "Mi-shell Mc-Dan-old"

She goes by "oneldammit" on instagram.

Michele McDannold is one of the best living poets in America, and we should all learn how to say her fucking name. She deserves it.

That is one of the little things society does that pisses me off. Butchers people's names like they don't matter. Kind of like how we mention Walt fucking Whitman invented free verse, and just forget all about Emily Fucking Dickinson. Kind of like how men have dominated the literature world for far too fucking long.

Life is cruel, and unjust, full of irritants, and humans

mostly don't make it better. That irritates the fuck out of me, too. It irritates Michele. Probably you, too, but Michele McDannold takes those irritants, the injustice, the human cruelty, and turns them into poems that sit heavy on your chest long after you've read them.

Life is cruel, and unjust, and it drives me fucking crazy. It probably drives you crazy, too. I've tried to be a good human, and I've tried to fight the good fight. I'm sure you have, too. I know you have. I'm tired, and you're tired, too.

Michele McDannold is tired. She's fought the good fight. She's been writing and publishing poetry, hosting art festivals and small press carnivals, and she's been foot to pavement, walking the talk, all the time and every day in the six-years I've known her. Ohhh, Michele is fucking tired. She's exhausted. But the book your holding is proof that's she's still fighting the goddamned fight. This book is proof that she doesn't know any other fucking way.

In the middle of all the fucked-up things going on in this crazy fucking world, Michele McDannold is still fighting to keep love and hope alive, in her own way, by writing poetry that turns the fuckery into poems of observation and prayer. You can hear the weariness between each line. Smell the hot, moist breath on the desperate primal screams of "why am I the only one that sees this shit?" The cries of "this is fucked. Let's do something." The prayers born of a stubborn refusal to give up on love, no matter how many times it has left us bloody and raw.

Lots of people turn rage into poetry, into art. It's a staple in every backdoor, two-bit dive bar coffee house reading. It's the main attraction in everything from literary academic magazines to back pocket punk rock zines.

And that's the thing that makes Michele McDannold's poetry so damned special. She turns rage and fight, bloody lips and taken advantage of hearts into poems that don't waste a single fucking word. Poems that belong in the prestigious brag-to-your-friends journals and scribbled in basement made zines.

Michele McDannold's poems by themselves are the combat boots of literature. Made for revolution, born of a fuck you I won't quit fighting spirit. Together, as a collection, they're like a sun-washed crystal in your right pocket. Smooth, shiny, and so comforting to carry around that you almost believe it's all gonna work out somehow.

"Mi-shell Mc-Dan-old." Say it right.

Dan Denton

12-21-21

CONTENTS

From a certain point onward there is no longer any turning back.
That is the point that must be reached.

— Franz Kafka

when progress is working your way back

the call came at a time of quiet panic, days of vinyl, solitude and warmth. turns out you can panic anywhere. faced with being stuck in a witness booth, a glass case — out of harm's way but in the thick of it, just the same. recording the events with heartbreaking precision. the most recent undoing, detached and yet tethered to another wreck. doesn't matter at that point if i caused it or not, past tipping and yet unsunk is no time to get analytical about it. 'actionable items only' is the mantra of the survivor. so the timing was perfect for that call ...

west coast notebook entry #9

today we go again.
birds chirping good morning
smoking a bowl on the sidewalk in oakland.
can i turn the hardest criminal to a smile?
i feel sort of naked about it
though it's difficult to imagine
anyone
much pays attention
outside of themselves.

it took a good three months
to figure out
the city.
please just keep on
please just keep keeping
for the various entities
how things get done

for me,
the break
and all the way down
is of no consequence

happy accident

(just here to read the books and hear the stories)

i haven't seen the hollywood walk of fame
disneyland or the chinese theatre
the street names seem familiar
from a movie, maybe
oh that one book
and the neighborhood names
some i know and clearly remember why

i'm told that if i meander down the wrong street
into the wrong section of town
well it won't be good
mexicans with machetes, they said back home
here, the explanation is simply a matter of territory

i'm taken with the history
the struggle
the resilience
and the sadness
that maybe this one little crack in the sidewalk
is all that remains of what once was…

i haven't seen the helicopters circling
or even one hooker of note
the random violence
of which i'm sure is here
as is anywhere else
none of that has happened yet

i saw the hollywood sign from a distance
craning my neck to glance it on a cross street
as we're blowing through this section
to the next

i don't know where i am
or where anything in relation to this is
that, i don't mind so much
sometimes getting lost is preferred
and i love seeing things i certainly didn't expect
but know
i already know
that i could never love driving these streets
and what the natives have forgotten
completely understandable, sure ...
still—not everyone dreams of coming to LA

pristine settings

we can sleep with the doors open to the LA air despite the smoggy edges probably worse for us than we realize. still, there is that energy. maybe it's the how and why of what we find viable. every man gets lost not to himself but to some collective. it feels like strength yet it is of another. today i get lost with the day of korean shopping malls. the bathrooms are good but i am fat in this world, if it matters.

just some mushy shit

dreaming of your arms but woke up freezing. into all the unspoken, in every language that there is — love is both the easiest and hardest to translate. il mio amore, such missness. sleep more now in my coat. maybe i need to reconsider my substitutions.

if only you could bottle it

if all i left him with
was a tshirt
i'm sorry
the finer points
must have been
well-missed, then

but somehow i doubt it

that entire album
the smell of that one shampoo
and if i can be so bold
a handful of moments
unique but not so rare
in how easy it was
between us

magical thinking 101

if i was at home where i belonged, i'd be taking a nap
right now. i'd have let the record player blare into
nothingness but a faint swish, swish, swish. i might
wake up feeling a bit lazy and a lot contented, switch
to an old cd and swipe the counters and tables and
whatnots of dust real quick before you're due home.
if the house had grown cold, i'd make it warm again
...tending to the unlit fires as if i had a say in it.

protect the innocents

there's a greediness that compels her moves. in the have-nots of the moment she's now unaware, leftover from a youth without choice or control. it's easier to place it in the material things, like vanity, the generous nature of 5-star comment cards. that hand up she's offering is only worth the least weight of pulling you down at the right moment. it's the trap door gag that nobody's laughing at. only the fake sad smile of a clown.

at the tee gee club #1

bob wants to hear metal

we fumble the
quarter
and change the language
to Spanish but
eventually he
gets it
three songs later
Planet Claire
Elvis Costello
and that one prince song
all the while his fifth wife
and a trip to the philippines

he gets his quarter
time for a smoke
because today the news

and knowing it's coming all along
doesn't grease the wheels for
Soundgarden
doesn't temper the pain for
Metallica even, old school

iris will watch my drink for me
top it off so i can
say i'm happy
so i can slip and say
i might not be ok

but you know i'll be fine

west coast notebook entry #13
if your process needs a mountain, go

it's very complicated.

possible i might
not come down
from this
highway crest
in the clouds
here comes the rain, just
a sprinkle

one could feel cold
save for the sun-direct
patches of light

you know what it
reminds me of?
as does everything
right now…

when i leave this
mountain
will i leave the memory
of you
here too?

tell me how

west coast notebook entry #23

the air up here though

oh goodness — these
people
so *faded* to
an alternate
demographic
hiking with Starbucks
in American Apparel
they brought their own
soundtrack
playing photo shoot
from a boombox in too good
a condition
to make any sense

an insurance commercial
a life stuck
on the share button

these
are genuine smiles
LET'S POST THIS

and they appear to stand closer
to the edge

**you're probably going to worry about the wrong
thing like bears or sodomites. so just don't worry**

taking my chances in bear country

remember which hand
you touched the door
with
remember the handi-wipes
next
time
remember that the fires burning
can be either a light to
follow back
or away

the fog rolls in

we're walking in a
cloud now

enough

abundance, it rains
on this sleepy saturday drought
cracks in the sidewalk
and everywhere else
filling up

it was there lurking
clouds heavy with promise
the somber and unrepentant jazz
the lips moments from the kiss
the sweet surrender
that lone trumpet sounding
the all-clear
the alright
with what we already had
right here

west coast notebook entry #4
helicopters don't have blind spots

i can't get a
moment
a patch of sky
a break

i can't get white to
turn black
or vice versa
& they're all out
of grey
can't get a good deal
but i sure
can't get whining
all too much about it

the sprinklers
are on
despite the drought

so many hands
that need washed

and as much as i'd like to
avoid
roundtable discussions
on the politicizing
of a social construct
the city won't quiet
its desperation to manipulate
borders within borders
within borders

studies show
even the helicopters
are in on it

west coast notebook entry #6

when you need to sit in a dark theatre, crying by
yourself, with others

you notice it's an everyday thing
you notice it's a three times a day thing
you notice that our last dollars
were maybe more important than all those other
dollars
you notice that the kid behind the counter, this one
anyway
still smiles in that not in spite of himself way
that us old-timers well that's all we're really
wondering about
you notice that when it's over
just enough time was burnt
to cast the perfect shade across the sky
you notice that the city needs more than
a mere spat of rain
to clear the air
& figure maybe
that's how the humans work too

steel reserve 211
high gravity

trading a brown bag beer
from the rite-aid
for a cold
one
in my sweater ...
i told you these are
important decisions.
gliding down sunset blvd
when the gradients are just right
the differently-abled humps her walker
at the bus stop
blowing devotions
at the moon sky
& all the while
that twinkle in her eye
a judgment on the navigational
misfortune
of too many things in a day
we are what we wish for hard enough

only in LA, baby
only in LA

west coast notebook entry #27
being so weird at the party

i have to wonder why the heck i'm here
oh you midwestern people,
aren't you so quaint.
oh you writer people,
aren't you so cute
with your angst & rebellion.

i sit next to a daddy gay
& learn about grindr
I'M CALLING THE POLICE AT MIDNIGHT
she screams
so i sneak out
rolling up the hollywood hills
squeezing through those streets
as if anyone could.
feed the feral pussies,
& touch one finger to the moon—
MTV will never be that way again,
neither will i.

west coast notebook re-entry poem #17
vagrant observations

if only all days
were the ways
in which
the rainbow propagates
into jumbo mouse ears.
wrought iron fences shaped to
hold the childhood in.
what sort of wicked porn
turned this into
a busty lustful waterfall moment
a wife-beater
wet w/ sweat moment
an are you joking me
about the avocados moment.
only in the absurd
does absolute purity
dine on skin flick

the center of the country pretends these margins do
not exist
while they're ogling all over it
while they're licking the sweat right off

it's an interesting slice of pie

lackluster ending

i need some sunscreen
i need a bag of lemons
i need to hear
a different bird
singing

but st. valentines
delivers none
of these
on this saturday afternoon

a walk in the sun
anyway

i think I'll have a margarita

navy days

ya know,
if you want a sad story,
i've got `em.
buckets full of guts —
yeah, tarred with cancer.
not your trick,
fine. pass `round the corner
to the seven guys I fucked for fun
it's not much when you think of seven
certainly not much to my man's 100s
but i'm a gurl.

and boy, he loves to tell them stories
`bout those fuckin' whores he did
back in the navy days
shootin' bananas out their twats
for fuck's sake!

yet i was tender once.
youth had it's way with my head
and a girlfriend too.
well, truth be told
it was mostly just
strawberry fields and electric blankets
but my truth is like mold
in our living room.

so it's all like
yes, cap'n
i'll play the shame
for that one —
in trades for this.

ahead of her class

woke up thinking about a-words
audacity
authenticity

sure sign that winter
will be setting in
soon

amorous
in a room of one's own

afraid (of …)

buscemi

he reminded me of buscemi
and everywhere it was this guy
how I didn't intend it
but I was watching
these random occurrences — well,
seemingly. how could it be that stacked
day on day, unrelated, related
a voice-over, a bit movie part
an old favorite
his cigarette dangles at me
you there, you
and this look-alike
how he was always going when
I was coming
to the grocery
around to the laundromat
I wanted to ask him
do you go cold or
risk the fade

friendly advice

find another way to make money
invent new ways to stalk your lover
start a diet fad
marry a rich man
kill em with your good looks
and big tits
don't take a penny
dig graves for a living
with your fierce competitive attitude
sell, sell, sell
aim high
shoot low
find an airfield saturated in hair spray
tell the whole world
about the mood you're in
in other words
lie, lie, lie

as halothane, procaine, or ether

go on with your life
do not become the poem
she will treat you
as an open wound
in a salt factory
mop the floors with you
needle and thread you
without anesthetic
posturing for a picture book
on how you should not do
a fine surgical maneuver
she will make you bleed
a little
enough
just enough to satisfy the page
though, in the end
it will mostly be
pain
for the sake of
pain
you will be left with
question after
question
tripping down the catwalk
under the fluorescent lights
under the footfall of man
day after day
after day
they live the thing you are
knowing not

Charlie don't Surf!

Axl rose is high on moon pies.
   He does Frankenstein bits for the pony show.
He confuses Manson with the Viet Cong,
   A chop-shop in the consciousness.
One quarter puts a man's face, flat on a penny.
   I had a summer like that once.
I wore a black hat every day, until
   I left it in the Topps Big Boy;
When they tore it down,
   The fever left me.

who are they

who are the real poets
who are the real people
did they sleep next to me last night
did they tumble from the face of the earth
before i woke
i found a blanket on me
it smelled like lovelies
i only dreamt of a phone call
there was a question
but i forgot why and where
and only this
was left

rules of the road when navigating a trip closet

enter with love
do not snap your fingers
& do not jump out of
the shadows, there is no
need
this is a closet outside
the closet
you are participating
without agenda
be
here

in a moment
we will all spin off
into the universe where rules
are sketchy and
not to be trusted, challenge
your assumptions
this is a safe space
with a pillow to rest
ur head
we are
whispering sweet
everythings in your
ear
no permission slip
required, liable
is a funny word

back by sometime still called monday

we travel by landmark and compass
an itinerary that
not only includes
but demands
getting lost

what's needed
is
highly re-evaluated

we have friends in every port —
some will pull through
and some will
forget what day it is

piss by the side of the road
carry various weaponry
but most importantly
always carry a can opener

you do have to know
a stranger when you see one

be careful out there
safe travels, all that

clues to watch out for are:
uniforms.
and anyone else sunk so low
all they have is
it's us or them ...
look for desperation
never forget crazy
and anyone thinking they

have/need/are
power.
the bloodlust riffs off them
loud as sirens, those ones

sometimes they come with smiles
but still
you usually know.

how to decide if something is triggering

the sound of a dog slurping water
is triggering
the accidental taste of grit,
triggering.
Aqua Net hairspray
& grape kool-aid
ruins me
for days.
the crisp
pronunciation
of
names that begin with
the letter C...
fuck, man.
if i had to sit in his lap again
all four years old and trembling,
blacking out in the worst parts —
it would torture and comfort me
for years to come.
well it would not do me any worse
for the detached i have come to learn.
but i love you anyway
and all the
mundane
sights, sounds and smells
that get me on a regular basis / +
a lawnmower in the distance,
the blackened room,
the smell of fresh, boiling
water

macha
for Dev

word for word

all of the waters
on a thursday night
there are legs
not at all shaky
and an attitude
sways like hips
in a rock n roll
desert scene

xmas shopping list: free hugs, check twice

today i consider my
xmas list
arrange the words in my head
that will explain why
i have no gifts
that will explain why
instead i'm printing up pages
worrying over cover art
regretting that last latte i
didn't need
wondering why i had to go so far
and beg for gas money
wondering why i ever did a fundraiser
to pay for a website
wondering why i gave all those books away
(but i know that one)
why i kept pushing that magical jeep
why i got others to push it with me
i mean, FUCK
i should have thumbed it
i should have followed the kids
& ran the jug around
stood waiting for the pickup truck
at the day labor
i should have taken up a
corner
and either gone
all-out krishna
or hey, look at my tits! ...
just some flesh that will
be gone
in barely a speck-view
of the universe.

Michele McDannold   33

my friend has cancer

reject the body.
further
reject the systems
that poison us every. day.
that disinterested glaze
slathered around all that
mind-numbing propaganda
hooked on the divide & conquer
as if television still only comes
in black & white
even the rednecks don't want that anymore

reject any life that is about consuming
to waste
the actual parts that make being a
human
make being alive
make the very air you breathe
in your they set em up you knock em down
doe-eyed slavery
the cutest sheen of
a wonderful life
you'll ever put a hashtag to

kids, i don't know.
i think about all this
think about this community
all those tiny hands full of fight
how life is just too damn hard on people sometimes
how you can't put those hands up to do anything
about it
if they're busy holding all those bags

let it go ...

hold on only
to what's
important

love you

and go down, in your own way

love is the X factor you can't fuck with

feel more
stockholm
folding into
a space
guaranteed
w/answers

ask questions
i can complicate

the truth is
midnight prayer

you're all a bunch of horrible animals

i come home tonight after many drinks
with friends of like mind
and still i am not consoled
and still i want to google
"how to make a molotov cocktail"
and use one

maybe fear the people like me
with some semblance of how to use the language
to affect
but good luck to anyone counting on that —
i'm not.

if you haven't a two for one special,
fuck off.

they will speak of admiration
and the oh so cute with your revolution
but listen here girlie
there is a better way ...

thank you, i am quite practiced
at the grin that gets me through

of all the things i fake upon the universe
this is the worst

i will keep telling my children — yes,
you can. demand it.
i will keep telling the poets, yes —
the world needs you.

the world fucking needs you!
and secretly hate that i am lying.
secretly hate that there is nothing
literally not a thing you can do about it
but rock on with your bad self.
PLEASE
PLEASE
PLEASE
rock on with your bad self.
FUCK! if absolution is what you seek,
let me pull out my big white power of knowing what
it means
to be an American — the only true
and native son
of an empire set on eating its young.
once again, GOD BLESS US, EVERYONE.

do not like this post
#i'll tell you why the poets

because i don't want to talk about the weather
because i don't want to talk about the latest episode of
because i don't know my place
because the odometer rolls over and another mile
begs
because get outside of yourself, be humbled and
exalted at the same time
because ya know, they're tricky
because words do sound better than that when they
spin and actually taste just fine with whiskey
because a good poet and editor will fix that last line
eyedrop of magic
spitshine formaldehyde
because we only get one life to be conscious about
because woke ain't no joke or hipster invention
because i have something to say and those fools on
the bus wouldn't listen
because avocado trees and rabid raccoons
because 4am rain
and because i can make coffee anywhere
while the heart stays tuned to that certain beat
i wonder if they know how much i love them
how much i need them
how much the world needs them
christ's sake, the ego —
tell no one, but listen.

Michele McDannold   39

you enjoy the privilege of
aka dear white dudes, bite it.

being in the room
presumed innocent
the control of everything

your indignance

the right to look
the right to touch
the right to
  take
    everything
anything your tiny little white male heart
desires

the right to mock

your foot on any neck
credence
authority
your own set of facts

the ease of the world
& the mothered arms of comfort
forgiveness
forbearance

the vulgarity of your denials

rape, pillage, plunder ...
women, children,
the meek & disenfranchised

you enjoy it all —

war, genocide, oppression
on a mass and all-encompassing scale

i tell you this
from the safety and comfort
of my own throne of whiteness
blinded by it
every sound of protest a pitiful whimper

do you find it unseemly?

write off the
whore, the heretic,
all simple-minded
well-meaning misunderstandings
of just how
things are
(meant to be)

you enjoy the privilege of
being
the center of the universe
a GOD
on this planet
across nations
across time
since the dawn of
time itself

with one damn rib
that prick Adam
bought the whole enchilada
and it's all yours

i'll wait for you to get it
over here

out of the way
cradling in my bosom
this delicious
red apple.

an accurate description of work yesterday

walked right up to that house full of pit bulls and tiki
torches
he's wearing a dress code that can be concealed but
today
it's warm &
the full sleeves, profane skin
all the wretched hate on display

how does this happen

smiled as he held the puppy
pleasant, more so than many
am i taller? this can't be
am i growing, is the floor sinking??

i am the most considerate out of body experience
we won't even tell anyone i am smiling
alice? where are you
please help

america, great again

he's not afraid to say nigger

he's not afraid to scream it out the window
across the lawn
and down the way
a serene landscape where no one flinches

he's not afraid to yell it in front of the children
in front of his wife
in front of god almighty and country
knowing fuck-all what it says to the world
let alone, the internal

and still he's spitting hate
like baseball players and chewing tobacco
like fathers beat their children out of duty
out of war-torn memories
collapsed mines
& a nickel in your bucket means anything

tonight your woman dies in a back alley abortion
& the angels rejoice

this is progress.
where you can buy your tiki torches
at the home depot,
armband of the disenfranchised
sold separately

somewhere
baby jesus is weeping

unequalibrium

only going to be responding in code from now on
as is how the universe
speaks to me
do poets we suspect
decipher but what if
we broke
detoxify the lives
can we speak violent, we
don't she
run the line into
a dead end street
your mom had a secret life where
you didn't exist

doppelganger

he reminds me of this boy
if not for a doppelganger, no
reason i would recall
brad, so sullen,
frail &
pissed
drives a 2-seater
and lives
just past that one bend in the road
a little too far out

curious things

i find curious connections
in strings
words
the dog
licking his paws
the way his head moves
bugs
these things make me
love
these things make me
sick

i wonder if i was
born this way
or was it like some
sci-fi movie
rubber-banded from a
corn field
one blank blue night
to a saucer full
of experimenting green men
with round protruding eyes

and . . .
why are they always men
exploring
while the women sit home
burning the midnight oils

i would burn oils
but anymore
they break them over my head
tell me i can't have a frying pan
in both hands

ladies aren't what they used to be
and the flying man is amused.

drop dead stop

running into drop dead stop —
it hurts, you know.

got a gumption to set myself on fire
but all the signs said "hell no" ...
go back the way you came,
so I ended up in that tiny place
droppin' like a damsel, i squirmed
i swore on fate another day
but she found me 'cross the aisle
in that nondescript truck stop
all that brought me was the neon signs
and no car. go, go, go.
not a second of misdirectognition —
but it'd been so long.

where will the story end?
another patron enters, another
messages to atoms, material moves
a plane, I am surely unaware of, working
the road turns, it bows.

silver duct tape

i found a crater in my hand
with your name on it.
i asked where you went,
it said nothing.

there's a new guy here.
he put a wad of gauze there,
lots of tape.
it was silver duct tape,
the kind I fixed my car with.
i was poorer than I am now,
which is not much.
i used to say it could fix anything.
we would laugh,
just laugh our silly heads off.
ha ha ha
ha ha

purchase

it's just past noon on a wednesday
the local gas station buzz
i have a pack of gum
a pack of reds
and a water
the news translates
my secret buried in a tomb
those children there
scurry past and ride off
into the sunset

engaging the dream

that morning
there were
four kittens
on the side of the road
not sure if
they were going
to stay or run
the morning was cold
avoiding last night's
puddles

in step
a mist of rain

you said things
i never wanted
to hear

i see the colors changing
like it's nothing
out of the ordinary

the blue
the very deep blue

the story behind this photo

will it ever be as if he never was?
thought perhaps one of us might
kill the other
in a fit of mad love
or at least so much living
for who dies first

the words are all the life beyond me
i have left to give
and it's just not enough

rather than being accidental

pretty sure the best laid plans
mean nothing
to the sharpie
on your name tag
to the misfitting sweater
and the comes in a package underwear
you are chipped nail polish
broadcast-live
crucifixion
unfiltered by design
the seed of doubt
mother nature uses to
reclaim
the broken
but there is no clean break
there is only sleeping at the wheel
bent
a contortionist running metal
burns one thing for another
the shelves are stocked
with gas ovens
and bottomless drops

take your pick, kitten
your secret is safe
with me

what a fuckin' life, right?

reduced to the
communications
over wires
across time zones

i cannot find
the map
that says

you
are
here.

there'll be time for that later

she began noticing everything
in her world was manilla-
colored. her skin had turned
manilla, the bare mattress on
sheet-changing days …manilla.
the very air filling that room.
yes, manilla. if her life
resembled anything at all, and
perhaps there are more
appropriate words for colors
seen and unseen, but i tell you—
it was every molecule, manilla.

the grainy
the slick
it all tasted the same

she contemplated gold,
soft light,
water shadows,
lampshades.
there is no sound
to manilla

all the laundry turned this color
all the lids
all the unwashed hands
and corners
and every
broken
thing

another layer of understanding

he thought she might be the devil
& she hoped maybe he was/
would be
for those times necessary
only
to take her apart
from the ties that bind
push her farther
onto the edges
where everything
drips
indigo blue ...
i know it doesn't make
any sense
but that was
the color
of her
dreams now

thanks for finishing it for me

the filthiness comes so very
naturally
inside his mind
and manifest via text
she is the only thing
that's bad about me
we're so good at delusions
and the long game
think of all the things
between here
and there
before we get caught
in something real

meeting a friend

that first night.

brought in from the rain,
from the dark ...
down old highways
over the bridged river.
windows — none,
and county roads
slimmer than one and a half
rugged tires
and fresh bug juice,
a constant current not
the kind that crackles
the kind that maintains.
air thick with it
does not move without
your motion.
cutting through
quite specifically,
navigated
to a bowling alley bar.
you, drunk
in from the chicago train,
already wearing your intended's ring
yet
fresh from a disappointing search
for another.
i suppose you figured
what the hell.
as did i.

step up your gift game with tips from pro wrappers
Bow not included

what do i write anymore
but epic craigslist masterpieces
that get flagged
for being impossible

actionable items only please

the holidays came and went
mourning for the dead
mourning for the living

we eat til it hurts
even if it already did

missed connections
misunderstandings

the world's a mess
but there's always
the clearance aisle

for him

things are rusty
after too much
running
running to
running away
the difference
becomes negligible
after a while

go ahead
& claim
sanctuary

just watch the fuck out
when it decides
to claim
you.

hazard is imminent

there are nine dimensions
of reality
happening
in this space
and time

we are
only three

diving in ocean surf, we
are
warning

multisensory delivery mechanism

in a sense, exact

just keep writing
sensory input
because i'm kind of
at a loss.
glass-encased
seeping heat
space, a bubble
the world turns outside only
twice a day
a snowglobe on a timer
what do we do with this time
as important
as any
oh yea?
there are holes in
the telephone pole out front
maybe a squirrel colony
it's a thin coat of vanilla
frosting
as far as the eye can see
any moment now
you'll be home
home
is that something i'm interested in?
like no other this
makes
perfect sense

tonight i need to let go

but he says
we have to stop
and his plan works
as i feel the disappointment
slide forward, all around
i can't shake it
like that landslide
song
you keep playing
over and over
and over
and you still don't
get the point

until the universe
has decided
i've learned this lesson
well enough

just watch ...
the sun rises red
but goes pink early
in the clouds
it doesn't take her long
to be done
look away
and you've
missed it

the choose your own adventure stories we tell ourselves

i'll start doing things
to get out of it—
burning a
hole in your
favorite t-shirt
ruining your
beautiful
record collection ...
then i'll remember
the only sound advice
my ex-husband
left me with

you're not required to do
anything in this life,
except die.

all i ever
wanted to write
was a happy ending

how to pull a curtain, no hands
alternatively, closure

when the smell
goes to afterbirth

when the song turns
to shudder

when the bags pack
themselves &

make a run for it
in the middle
of the night

that chapter
is called
goodbye

point of departure

it was february 7th, 2015. no colder than any days
before, remembered. crisper, maybe. when there has
been snow and retaining temperatures most often
accompanied by grey days then you get a break like
this morning sun before the warm reaches and melts a
thing, one could look out over the flattened cornfields
of illinois running into the horizon, the vanilla icing
top layer thin that makes that noise when your shoe
pops down to powder and still you might think you
could work up a good slide and just whoosh off into
forever...

this was the point of departure that would turn into
12 of the 15 states i traveled to in 2015 from february
to may. for the miles, i'd have to check the record.
admittedly, it was the least anticipated, planned or
organized journey. just to say that my intention was
to make it count.

you have to stop calling me momma

if only i had a working uterus ...
i could birth nations of ___

(and thus begins the problem)

un-gender specifics
breed them sweet
with dirty hands

that smell of lanterns
that smell of lilac falling
common denominator =s beat

chipless wonderers that eat the heads of consumption
the line is too long

the thought is diluted
my babies write poems to burn in a stolen fire
campside, along the cold desert night

not really here today
nor gone tomorrow

if somehow we didn't

have wings that clip
to the black surface
of our waking lives
we might soar
instead of
stutter
at the light
ahead
we might
take that road
into night
unknown
with less trepidation
than ever before

they say
she is not afraid
like it's a bad thing
when they are really bold
they say
she is fearless
in a tone unkind

and quite noticeably
envious

softly i regret to tell you

off in the distance a muffled rumble, close. your eyes.
& it.
(do you hear that)
w i l l   v i b r a t e   * t h r u *

don't.
depend.
too hard.
on the adj.
ectives

time is no longer now, fetching for a better view
these babies will be brighter than the rest

our modern dilemma,
the message in the bottle not lost at sea — preserved
forever
and no one

digressing is a
good way to …

will early morning cold always remind me

waking up there
in your body warmth
running downstairs
with the cats to
turn the heat
and the music on

the sun rising
the ease of it all

the clarity

many things

but that
i have not felt
since

plainsong

i am thinking about your place
this cold of winter
this time of day
the sunshine warm
slowly receding
to other glows

years later,
it warms me still.

the extent to which i am floored

off the ground
your love is
too stream of consciousness

isn't it the usual that
fire on a fragile thing
will break

or is it reinforce

what is the most tactile
word you feel
I can't choose between luxurious
& pornographic

you know
when you meet someone who understands
the mechanics of your body
and your mind

i should run
as they say
these things never work out

but today
we meet on the river that
runs contrary to the norm
one of five in the states
says the landlady

the idea

to go beat was the idea
find limits by pushing past
live the art you are going to make
in the decoding process
we all give in

i forgot how to write
& remembered it is just letters
to the best in us willing to listen &
when there's no one there
aren't we forced then
to learn the most

42 trees in a line at this
nutto cement patchwork, anchor-themed retreat
people care here
which is strange for a place
where one goes to be unnoticed

the basics of the superstition
breaking light bulbs 2 at a time

something lost
     something found

how to unbecome

protect your magic
claws
anti-theft planet
(at the end of the
rabbit hole)
          poised

when the road ends
here
this is
where i'll be

putting things where they
belong

unraveling extension cords

sweeping
under the rug

origin of casual
burn this one

the poem where he
meets her
on a bench
at a place
we will never
learn to pronounce
correctly

the walls
drenched in
gasoline —
a lighter
he hands to her.

here you go,
sugar.

burn this one

when he brings me lighters
easy does it with that fire

the non-stop air
is good
setting of alarms
is good
in the mid-day
blues playing
shade drawn
afternoon of him,
life is good.

i barely made it to
presentable,
chores
and nervous energy.
all wasted at the door
as he steps in.

this is the life now
and soon
dinner somewhere
with just the right
breeze
& lighting

to the puzzling situation which seems to involve a contradiction
can i get that martini to go

sitting in the rain
outside the eats
it's too loud
in the bar
with the fancy
people & the
prime rib

i go outside
down the way
to the benches
where nobody sits
with the outstanding
shrubbery & art-
etched sidewalk
that no one notices

the leaves sound off
to another year
all dry and crumbly
going on their way, i
wonder what
the world will mean
tomorrow

the sound of tread on
wet pavement
the smell of winter
coming
of finding a place
to stay for a spell

the other diners shudder by

in their quicksand agenda
i hear the last tale of flip flops
hitting the autumn concrete

it should be a new
moon tonight
the holidays loom
in the next weeks
& we shall see
if all is good

show me

this climate to another
time zone
does the news
& weather report
wreck your hair a different
product placement
at 3am
last week we played
telephone
and the strings
they seared
to your lover's eyebrows
and i
lost in the skydrive
lost in the ether
of words at trainstops

pics or it didn't happen
pics or it didn't happen

at the buffalo

good morning in the still dark

edgy shadows
damp remembrance of yesterday
reporting live from the
drop-in motel
where a combination of
roadside picnics
(comforting if not serene)
& sad domestic situations
occur
simultaneously

expired honey returns
to her room with
package in tow
maybe it's work
maybe it's the kind of work
polite society wouldn't speak of

i keep watch out of the periphery
wonder if the chinese take-out is okay
without refrigeration
it smells like an
alcoholic's wet dream in here
on the margins
but this space in the middle
where it's all warm without a single fuss
where it's all your scent and mine lingered together
on the bed sheets
where the effectiveness of a single yessss
causes the bedside alarm clock to crackle
uncontrollably
it's probably responding to some bizarro frequency

i forget your name
i forget mine
it is
the best

if i told you

you wouldn't believe me
so i just poem it

where the sound of
to blur
the voice
reaches cataclysmic
rendering

you know the one
over crackled phone
over a shallow breath
of yet uncalculated risk

if only the lines
curved right
at the
dial tones

a confession
straight ahead

in that all matters complicate and refine

the morning sun +
daybreak's cigarette smoke
fill the room.
his drawers on the floor
where i left them last night

it's been months since
i could even breathe a poem (prayer)
tried communing with those clown car gods — the poets
they had both good & silly things
to say about love, life
and the great & sad state of humanity

i breathe fire, she said
i'll swallow that whole, he replied

ever walk into a bar only to become
witness to an intervention?
the tiniest thing rules the entire room

now the scent of bacon
& gear sounds, shifting on down the road
the waning summer wind already too cold with the lake effect

i'll watch the leaves turn from this window

turn in my seat —
i can touch the palm of your foot
i can dwell in the chest of your heart
soft like pudding
or play-doh,
i haven't decided which.

purposeful interaction theory
soon the day comes

in the cold air
now prepped
for a storm
the trucks gathering
anything left not dead
dies soon
& all the whole day is gloom
inside impending clouds
long after the train, the wind
trails gone into
a tunnel
who is to say
how long these signs
are just a pictograph
of curious patterns
and mismatched currents

cityscapes while sitting on a cold, cold stone

it's been a full day
business + reminisce,
lake shore & shoreline.
the city ...
it costs to walk the streets here.
unnoticed is unpaid ...
not everyone has a dream beyond
a warm meal and a safe bed.

street gospel thaws a pedestrian
every 6 or 7 turns.
that's not too bad
but it's not too good either.

can you tell me where the yellow brick road goes
when unaccompanied by
red sequined shoes?

there is a home in the heart of
every traveler, she thinks
as he walks away
pretending
to save her number
& she knows
& she smiles relief
to the tips
of her
toes

found mister d #7
gas station dialogue

no problem —
have a good night
tires are washed out
clutch is sticking
dr pepper, not much
else is clicking
their dad needs his lotto cards
pays with a roll of quarters
he goes back in one more time
the sixth

the winter wears on

i'm getting fat
& you
are getting mean
there is no
dog to hunt
or even sleep
at the foot of the bed
there lies only
a dream

when will the sun shine again

but he don't know what it means

it appears like nagging
this unrestrained desire for more
give me
give   me
give
     me

the setting is a room
with soft white walls
a flowered plant in various
stages of bloom, charming in all
from ripe to waning ...
fresh air, billowing
the curtains into your space,
knocking things over and
snuffing out the candlelight

if one could direct the flow of energy
would not one shut the fucking window?

love

soon my teeth will fall out
and the broken glass on the floor
will get cleaned up
how on earth can a mind be unrest
while dealing in such certainties
i walk the dogs
i prepare a meal
things are folded with nary a thought
i'll cradle this one little word until i die
even if it kills me

walk in your shoes, boy

you bought them

they are all so pretty
and waiting
just
for you

game over

why can't we just be friends? why can't i just continue to put my penis in you? why can't you exist in a sphere with no emotions? why can't you just be my mommy? why can't you just take it, hard? harder? why can't you just let me take care of you? why can't you just need me all the time for everything but actually not too much? why can't you forget the weight of a word like love? why can't you suspend truth? let's play.

the science of breaking up
taken down by you

removed from the planted feet
on shaken ground
but i was at steady
and there you are with your pinholes
irrational, sweet little desires
that they are
a worked-over poem can be good
but can it be honest
i wish i could speak of the stars
or a hummingbird, landing it fierce
and new on your ears, still
saying something …
weighty.
the words would be of sinew, sinewy
and yet there is no meat
a connected emptiness, related
this dissipated space to the next
don't you know you fall through such tangles?
don't you know nothin' at all

when she figures out it's not a love story —
love story resolutions

let her go.

regret is for the
moon dust
she leaves behind
somewhere there
in the days you spent

akin to the last rays
at sunset
to the kiss
that lingered
longer than it lasted ...

simple question

i loved him as much as he would let me
how much does this heart weigh now

imposterization

the city creeps
the night screams
it's all so noir
and smudgy —

stand next to something
real, maybe
you are
projecting

maybe somewhere else
but not here
the city here gnaws on itself
the only sound you hear is
look who's over there ...
look who's looking
look

porch sessions #1

i am the tired of bones
tossed at sea &
washed up in a nether land

i should find what makes for bones
or become an adornment
or a pulverized mix of things
meant for something special and mysterious…

like love
oh love
oblivious to coercion
does it wait on untended beaches
for washed-up things?

destiny is the trust of waves
and do you know what that looks like?

**while thinking about all those suicidal adults and
your own relative story**
porch sessions #2: survey

pause
for a moment
focus on the why
a 2 month old child
might be referred to
CPS.

an acronym meaning
fucked
from the get-go.

you think i sell them short?
i don't.

some are mistaken
and some will
pull through anyway,
some
     how

pull that focus back in
((SEE THE BABY))

cradle their head in your hands
check the head circumference.
do the eyes follow the light?
the sound of your voice?
when you stretch out those little legs,
how far do they go?
can you measure their weight
in your arms?
step onto the scale

& tell me.

check once,
twice,
three times…

this assessment will be over in approximately
90 minutes.

that's really all the time we have
thank you for your input

a number of various things today
porch sessions #3

watched a flower slowly bloom
from the front porch
it takes a long time
it's still not done
i felt, once again,
the blooming of heartache
surround my lungs
and settle in.

it takes a long time
it's still not done

quietly destructive things
a person whom the speaker dislikes or despises

is how i get fat and bad haircuts
is how bad men
"get" me

examinations

thank you
for the tiny metal implements, sharp
digging into torn flesh
furrow out black misshapen bits of rock
gravel lodged in various degrees like maggots
burrowing deep

are you pregnant with it
bleeding no part
now i walk this path
my own
wounds wrapped
tight like oats, thick.
come in capsules. why
do we
come in veils

spacetime continuum for dummies

it took me five days
to realize why i was
so depressed
the anniversary
of the day we met
some years ago, now
different everything

i didn't notice the date…
keep track of the day of week
by what everyone else
around me
is doing

soon there'll be
a new anniversary
though i forget the date
the last time i saw you

we'd spent the night
in a white trash
ghetto
airbnb
played pool for most the hours
set a grill on fire
pretended to fish
i washed the dishes
and after
we just laid there
talking quietly
about the times
good, bad, and ugly
holding hands
like a couple of junior high kids

tick of clock
tick
tick
tick

in the morning
we did not say goodbye

we had a fit
like no other,
a love affair
to match

i guess
that'll have to
be enough

"Michele McDannold is a literary rebel and this irreverent, delicious book, her best yet, is proof. McDannold has a way of stripping everything down to its essentials, leaving the reader sated, and yet with a strange sense of longing. "i guess/that'll have to/ be enough" the poet says in the last line of the final poem of this fine collection. Indeed." — Alexis Rhone Fancher, author of *Erotic, New & Selected*, poetry editor, Cultural Daily

"Michele McDannold's *By Plane, Train, or Coincidence* is a book that takes you to L.A. and lets you get lost in the gritty, quiet moments of a big city. She dials in on what happens to the mind in the desert, how all that space is damaging to the heart and mind if you are from somewhere in the Midwest. It's a book about what happens when a heart sets itself free, gets knocked around, and goes home to the memories of what love used to look like. There is a lot of emotion and raw views about being in love in McDannold's collection, but you'll have to pick through the shadows and candor to find it. When you do, it will hit you squarely in the jaw." — Aleathia Drehmer, author of *Running Red Lights* (Gutter Snob Books)

"If you're looking to explore your deepest dreams, Michele McDannold can walk you through the jungle they hide in. She unwinds the truth of the day's ragged edge, while allowing the magic of the good night to breathe deep – one last time. McDannold truly leads the life of a seasoned writer. She knows things, she shares them here. Her latest book – *By Plane, Train or Coincidence*. I like it. Lots." — Bill Gainer, *A True Story*

"McDannold's mastery of language thrives raw and unsparing in *By Plane, Train or Coincidence* ...lines living in "a city that gnaws on itself". With pathos, humor, and her driving fearlessness she transforms any landscape into languid rhythms of fertile hauntings. She is a phenomenon, a fierce visionary. Get a copy of anything she writes!" —Meg Tuite, author of *White Van*

"Michele McDannold's *By Plane, Train or Coincidence* hits powerfully deep. A touching collection of sparking, popping, hissing poems shot out like fireworks over the real world below." —Bud Smith

www.ingramcontent.com/pod-product-compliance
Lightning Source LLC
Chambersburg PA
CBHW031902090426

42741CB00005B/610